Looking after
Gerbils

Laura Howell

Designed by Joanne Kirkby
Edited by Sarah Khan
Illustrations by Christyan Fox

Consultant: Jackie Roswell

Usborne Quicklinks

For links to carefully chosen websites where
you can find out more about gerbils, go to the Usborne
Quicklinks Website at www.usborne.com/quicklinks
and enter the keywords **"pet guides gerbils"**

There you'll find links to websites where you can:

- discover the right pet for you
- watch video clips on how to care for gerbils
- find fun things to make and do
- discover fascinating facts about gerbils

Usborne Publishing is not responsible for the content
of external websites. We recommend that young children
are supervised while on the internet and follow the safety
guidelines displayed on the Quicklinks Website.

Contents

What is a gerbil?

Gerbils are small, mouse-like animals with hairy tails and strong back legs. They are clean, fun-loving and make excellent pets. This book will tell you what you need to know about buying and taking care of your first gerbil.

Appearance

Gerbils are about 10cm (4in) tall – larger than a mouse, but smaller than a rat.

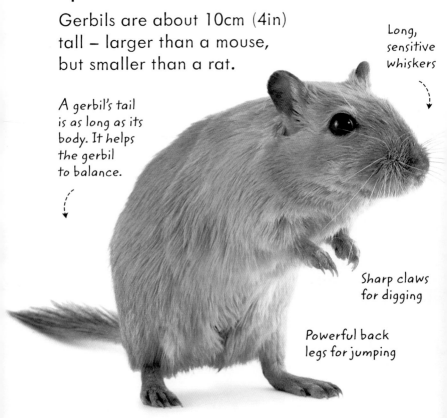

Long, sensitive whiskers

A gerbil's tail is as long as its body. It helps the gerbil to balance.

Sharp claws for digging

Powerful back legs for jumping

Desert diggers

Wild gerbils come from deserts and grasslands. They dig huge networks of tunnels where they live in groups called colonies.

The entrance to a gerbil's tunnel is only big enough to let a gerbil through. Most enemies are too big to fit.

Need to gnaw

Like rats and hamsters, gerbils are rodents. These are animals with two pairs of strong front teeth for gnawing. The name "gerbil" comes from "jarbu" which is the word for "rodent" in Arabic.

Gerbils and other rodents gnaw things to keep their teeth from growing too long.

Seeing

Gerbils can see better than people in dim light, but they have trouble seeing things close up, or in great detail.

A gerbil's eyes are designed to work best in weak morning and evening light.

Hearing

Gerbils have excellent hearing. When they stand up on their back legs and hold their heads high in the air, they are listening to what's going on around them.

Loud noises frighten gerbils, so keep your pet's cage in a quiet spot.

Smelling

Gerbils use their keen sense of smell to find food and identify friends and enemies.

Two gerbils meeting for the first time will sniff each other, to see if they are friendly.

Whiskers

A gerbil uses its whiskers to detect obstacles or to tell if a gap is wide enough to fit through. Its whiskers are the same width as its body, so if they fit through, the rest of the gerbil will too.

This gerbil used its whiskers to measure the width of the tunnel before crawling inside.

What will I need?

Try to have your gerbils' cage set up with the things they need before getting your new pets. You can buy these things from a good pet store.

A hideaway

Gerbils need a private place to hide. Sometimes they hide in their nest, but it's better if they have a nesting box. This should be made of earthenware or wood, as plastic will be chewed.

An earthenware plant pot like this makes a snug gerbil hideaway.

Some shredded paper towel will make the hideaway comfortable.

Nesting material

Gerbils make nests to sleep in. Before buying nesting material from a pet store, check the label to see if it is safe for gerbils. Fluffy materials, such as cotton balls, could choke your gerbil.

If you put some toilet tissue in your gerbils' cage, they will shred it into a nest.

Bedding

Gerbils are natural burrowers, so they need lots of material to dig around in. Wood shavings, corn cob and straw are all suitable. Don't use sawdust or cedar shavings, as they can cause infections and breathing problems.

You can use sand as bedding, but it's more difficult to clean out, and must be kept damp.

9

Food bowls

You'll need a large, ceramic bowl for fresh and dried food. Plastic bowls are likely to get tipped over, and can be dangerous for your gerbils if they chew them.

A heavy ceramic dish is harder to tip over than a plastic one.

Toys

Gerbils love to try out new toys. You can buy a range of gerbil toys from pet stores (see pages 48–49), but even the cardboard tube from a toilet tissue roll will provide lots of fun.

Don't clutter your gerbils' home with lots of toys. Two or three at once is enough.

This water bottle is positioned at a comfortable height for the gerbil to drink.

water bottle

Use a drip-feed bottle for your gerbils' water, and attach it to the side of the cage or tank. Don't use a bowl, as your pets will quickly make it dirty with bedding and droppings.

A gnawing block

A gerbil needs something hard to gnaw, or its teeth will grow too long. Blocks of hard wood sold in pet stores are safest for this. Any block of clean, hard wood is suitable, though, as long as it has a smooth surface and isn't painted.

Gerbil homes

Gerbils are very active and like to dig, so need space and suitable materials to make tunnels. They can be kept in a cage or a glass tank.

Cages

A pair of gerbils need a cage at least 60cm (24in) long and 25cm (10in) wide. The more gerbils you have, the more room they need.

A multi-level cage has more space for playing and climbing than an ordinary one.

The gerbils can dig in the bottom part of this cage and eat and drink in the top part.

Make sure the cage has closely
spaced bars that are unpainted.
Keep it where other pets, such
as cats, can't reach it.

*Make sure other
pets can't knock
over or jump up
on the cage.*

Plastic cages

Gerbils can live in a plastic cage designed for
hamsters, as long as it's big and sturdy enough.

*This picture shows
a multi-part
plastic cage.*

*The parts can
be dismantled
and rebuilt in
different ways.*

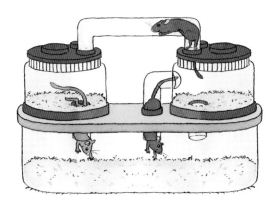

Your gerbils will enjoy running through the
tunnels and rooms, but you must make sure
that they don't chew through the plastic.

A gerbilarium

The best home for your gerbils is a large fish tank. Your pets won't be able to chew it like a plastic cage. You can fill it with bedding for them to build tunnels. A glass tank used to house gerbils is usually called a gerbilarium.

This gerbilarium has been adapted to have many levels. You don't need one like this, though – a plain fish tank is fine.

You can fix a water bottle to the top or side of the gerbilarium.

The tank should be at least one-third full of bedding material.

Keeping covered

It's important to make sure you keep a lid on the top of the gerbilarium, or your gerbils will be able to jump out.

A solid cover won't let in enough air, so use wire mesh attached to a frame made of wood or metal.

Staple chicken wire to a wooden frame to make a cover for your gerbilarium.

Staying cool

Keep the gerbilarium out of direct sunlight and away from radiators. The glass will trap heat and quickly make conditions too hot for your pets.

Too much heat can be very dangerous to small animals.

Choosing gerbils

It's best to buy your gerbils from a recommended pet store or breeder, who can tell you their exact age and also whether they are male or female.

What to look for

Here are some signs to look out for that show if a gerbil is healthy and happy.

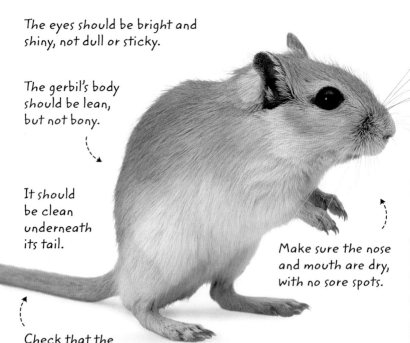

The eyes should be bright and shiny, not dull or sticky.

The gerbil's body should be lean, but not bony.

It should be clean underneath its tail.

Make sure the nose and mouth are dry, with no sore spots.

Check that the tail is long and straight, with no breaks or kinks.

A healthy gerbil will be active and curious.

How old?

Your gerbils should be six to eight weeks old
when you buy them. They are easier to tame
at this age. Before six weeks, they are
too young to leave their mother.

*A breeder will not separate baby gerbils
from their mother until they are ready.*

How many?

Gerbils don't like to live alone, so it's better to
buy more than one. A pair, or a small group
from the same family, will live together happily.
Make sure they are all male or all female, or
they will have lots of babies.

Females prefer to be in pairs.

Males live happily in groups.

Mongolian gerbils

There are around 90 types of gerbils, but only a few are kept as pets. Mongolian gerbils were originally bred in laboratories, but because they were so friendly and easy to take care of, they soon became popular as pets.

Jumbo jirds

Recently, people have also started keeping jirds as pets. Jirds are larger relatives of gerbils – they are about the size of a rat or small squirrel.

These are jirds. They have chubbier bodies and longer ears than Mongolian gerbils.

Buying a gerbil

When you go to the pet store, spend a little while just watching the gerbils in their home.

Decide which ones seem the most friendly and energetic. Ask if you can see them being handled.

Ask for help to check the sex of the gerbils you choose.

Don't buy female gerbils that have been living in a cage with males. They might have babies.

Settling in

A new pet needs time to get used to its new home. The next few pages will show you how to help your gerbils settle in.

Coming home

Your gerbils will be put in a box when you buy them. Ask to take some of their bedding for their new cage.

A handful of bedding with a familiar scent is comforting for a gerbil.

Take your gerbils straight from the pet store to their new home.

If you have a tank, place the box inside and let the gerbils run out. Remove the box, and put the top of the tank back on.

For a cage, hold the box over the open door, so the gerbils can jump inside. Close the door.

Setting up

Have a full water bottle and a day's worth of food ready in your gerbils' cage when they arrive. Ask the breeder or pet store what food they are used to eating, and buy the same kind.

Early days

Once you have put your gerbils in their cage, leave them alone for a day or two. They need this quiet time to get used to the sights and sounds of their new surroundings.

A toy, like this wooden castle, will make your gerbils' home more interesting.

This gerbil is being offered a juicy raisin by its new owner.

Making friends

At first, your gerbils will be cautious. Talk to them often and give them small pieces of food, so they know that you're their friend.

After a few days, offer food in the palm of your hand. By now, your gerbils should be relaxed enough to step onto your hand to eat. This helps them to get used to your touch.

Keep your hand still while your gerbil takes food from it.

Avoiding bites

Gerbils only bite when they are very nervous or annoyed. Don't tease your gerbils by poking your fingers through the cage bars.

Gerbils don't like to be grabbed roughly.

Try not to make quick, jerky movements or loud noises when you are near your gerbils. Never try to grab a gerbil suddenly.

Don't shout at your gerbil or punish it, even if it does bite. This will scare it, and might make it more likely to bite you again.

Feeding

Gerbils need a mixture of dried gerbil food, water, fresh vegetables and protein. There's more about fresh food on pages 28–31.

Dried food

Dried gerbil food contains a mix of things that are good for gerbils, such as dried peas, nuts and seeds. Food pellets contain the same sorts of ingredients ground up and pressed into chunks.

This gerbil is enjoying some sunflower seeds. You can give them as an occasional treat.

If your gerbil eats too many sunflower seeds it can become overweight.

Gerbil food mixes can contain these ingredients:

Sunflower seeds

Pumpkin seeds

Corn

Peanuts

Crushed dried peas

Gerbil food pellets come in different shapes and shades, but they are all made of the same things.

Storage

To keep your gerbil food fresh, store it in a container with a lid, in a cool, dry place.

Throw food away after three months, or it will no longer be safe for your pets to eat.

Unsafe snacks

Never give a gerbil sugary foods, such as chocolate, or anything spicy or salted. All these things are bad for your pet.

Rich foods can make a gerbil fat, or sick.

Changing diet

For variety, you could try giving your gerbils a new kind of food mix.

Introduce new food gradually, or your pets might get an upset stomach.

On the first day, start by mixing about one quarter of the new food with three quarters of the old food.

If you find a type of food that your gerbils really like, there's no need to change it for another.

Gradually add more new food and less old food over a 10-day period, until your gerbils are eating only the new food.

How much?

A gerbil needs a full tablespoon of food, given at the same time each day. If it keeps leaving lots of uneaten food, try giving it less. Throw the leftovers away at the end of the day.

Foraging

Your gerbils might scatter their food about and pick out the pieces they like best. This is called foraging. In the wild, animals forage to find things that are safe for them to eat.

Watch your gerbil picking through its food and see if you can spot which types it likes best.

27

Fresh food

A small amount of fresh food is good for gerbils. Give your pets fruits or vegetables at the same time as you give them dried food.

Apple

Gerbils usually like these foods.

Radish

Broccoli

Raisins

Carrot

Parsley

Never give onions, lemons or oranges, or watery fruits such as melon and cucumber.

Fruit frequency

You should only feed your gerbils fruit once or twice a week, or they might get sick.

Preparing the food

Wash fruits and vegetables thoroughly in cold water before you give them to your gerbils. Dry them off, then remove the peel and seeds.

How much?

Give your gerbils no more than two pieces of fresh food per meal, in small chunks. Throw away any that haven't been eaten at the end of the day.

You can put fresh food in the same bowl as dried food, as shown here.

Water

Gerbils don't drink much, but they still need a regular supply of water. Fill the water bottle with fresh water every day.

Hang the bottle so it doesn't touch the bedding, but not too high, or your gerbils won't be able to reach the spout.

Vitamins and minerals

Pet stores sell vitamin and mineral powders for gerbils that can be added to their food. Check the label to see if your gerbils' food contains them already.

If a gerbil looks well and has a varied diet, it probably doesn't need extra vitamins.

Treats

Only buy treats for
your gerbil that are
designed for rodents.
Many are made with
rich ingredients, so only
give them occasionally.

Treat sticks contain things
like raisins, popcorn and apple.

Protein

To stay healthy, gerbils need to eat food
containing protein. The easiest way to add
protein to your pets' diet is to give them a
little cooked egg or chicken.

This gerbil is
about to enjoy
a small piece of
boiled egg.

Gerbils don't
need added
protein often
— once every
two weeks is
enough.

Keeping clean

Gerbils are naturally clean, but their cages, bowls and bottles still need cleaning regularly, even if they don't smell bad or look dirty.

Every day

Remove all uneaten food from your gerbils' food bowl, and rinse it out before putting more in. Empty and refill the water bottle.

Every week

Replace the nesting material from your gerbils' cage. You only need to change the bedding once a month.

Nesting material and bedding can become stale if it isn't changed regularly.

This gerbil has been shredding its new nesting material.

Every two months

Clean out the cage.
Keep your gerbils in a
carrying box or bucket.
Put the metal part of
the cage over the top.

*Make sure the top of
the bucket is covered, or
your gerbils will jump out.*

Use hot water and
mild dishwashing
liquid to clean the
water bottle, food
bowl, toys and
cage bottom.

Rinse everything
off with clean water
and dry it thoroughly
with an old towel.

*Have a towel that's only used
for drying your gerbils' things.*

Tank cleaning

Clean your gerbils' tank every three months.
Tank cleaning can be messy, so take it
outside. Wash, rinse and dry it thoroughly.

*Ask someone to
help you take the
tank outside for
cleaning.*

Return the tank to its normal spot, then put
in fresh bedding. Clean the food bowl
and water bottle and put
them back too.

*Press the bedding
down firmly, so your
gerbils can make
sturdy tunnels.*

Dust baths

In the desert, a wild gerbil will give itself
a dust bath. It rolls around in the sand,
rubbing grease off its fur.

*Every few weeks, give your
gerbils some sand in an old dish,
so they can bathe themselves.*

Grooming

You don't need to wash or brush your
gerbils. They clean themselves by licking
their fur and running their claws
and teeth through it,
like a comb.

*This gerbil is
using its claws
to groom
its face and
whiskers.*

What does it mean?

Gerbils use movements to let each other know how they feel. If you watch your pets, you can learn what their body language means.

Winking

Gerbils wink when they are happy, and as a way of saying hello. If you wink at your gerbil, it might wink back.

If your gerbil winks at you, give it a treat.

Face to face

When two gerbils meet, they will usually touch noses or lick each other's mouths to prove that they are friends.

These gerbils are saying hello by touching noses.

That's mine!

Gerbils have a scent gland on their tummies. The gland makes an oil that only gerbils can smell. They will rub the oil on anything that belongs to them.

Scent gland

A gerbil's scent gland is a narrow patch of bare skin on its tummy.

Dig, dig, dig

If you see your gerbil digging furiously in the corner of its cage, don't worry. Gerbils love to dig in anything they can, so it doesn't necessarily mean your pet is trying to escape.

Gerbils can't resist the urge to dig in the corners of their home.

Look out!

Gerbils stamp their feet when they sense danger. The sound warns other gerbils to be on their guard. Males also stamp their feet when excited.

THUMP THUMP

An anxious gerbil makes a drumming noise with its feet.

I'm scared

Occasionally, you might hear your gerbil give out a loud, screechy squeak.

Gerbils only make this noise when they are scared or angry. A scared gerbil will also stand still, with its front paws held up.

Frightened gerbils stand frozen on the spot, like this.

Gnawing bars

Gerbils gnaw constantly to keep their teeth worn down. They will gnaw on anything hard. If your gerbil keeps gnawing on the bars of its cage, though, it might be bored.

Make sure your pet has something safe to chew, or it might hurt itself by biting the cage bars.

Give your gerbils some toys to play with, and a tough wooden gnawing block.

Licking

If your gerbil is licking the sides of its tank, it may be trying to drink moisture from the glass. Check that there are no blockages in its water bottle.

Licking glass is often a gerbil's way of telling you it's thirsty.

Handling

If you want to make friends with a gerbil, you must give it lots of attention and handle it regularly. Provided you're gentle, your pets will enjoy being held in your hand.

Timing and preparation

Don't wake a sleeping gerbil to play with it — choose a time when it's already awake. Before you take your gerbil out of its cage, check that there are no holes in the walls and floor of the room. Keep all other pets out.

Don't disturb your gerbils if they look sleepy.

Picking up

Approach your gerbil from the front, so you don't startle it. Slowly put your hand inside the cage.

Keep your hand still until the gerbil approaches it.

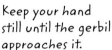

Let the gerbil sniff your fingers. If it's happy, it will come closer, or even run onto your hand.

Scoop the gerbil up using one hand on each side of its body. Gently hold it in your cupped hands.

Hold your gerbil over a soft surface, such as a cushion, in case it jumps or falls.

Hands off!

Most gerbils don't like having their stomachs touched. Only stroke your gerbils on their back or head.

Stroke your gerbil's back gently, as shown here, to help it feel relaxed.

Make sure you don't squeeze your gerbil.

Exploring

When your gerbil is comfortable being handled, help it get to know you better by allowing it to run up your arm and on your shoulders. Kneel down to do this, in case it jumps off.

Meeting friends

If your gerbils are completely tamed, they won't mind if other people handle them. Show your friends and family the right way to pick up and hold a gerbil before they handle them.

Help others when they are handling your gerbil, to make sure they do it correctly.

Tails of woe

Never pick a gerbil up by its tail, especially the tip. You might pull the fur tuft off, or even snap the end.

OUCH!

Gerbils have very sensitive tails, which are easily damaged.

Friends and enemies

A pair or group of gerbils will be best friends if they have always lived together. But if a gerbil meets a stranger, they are very likely to become enemies.

Gerbils who are friends, like this pair, will sleep, play and eat together.

Other pets

Although gerbils like company, don't keep them in the same cage as a hamster, mouse or other small pet. They have different habits and will probably fight.

Fighting

If you have to handle fighting gerbils, wear thick gloves for protection.

Gerbils fight standing on their back legs. Their fur bristles, and they box with their front paws.

Keep an eye on your gerbil to look for signs of fighting.

If it's losing weight and has bite marks on its body, your gerbil might no longer be friends with its cagemate.

Two gerbils who have had a fight must live in separate cages afterwards.

Gerbils that have fought won't ever make up and become friends.

45

Keep away

Once a gerbil has decided that it owns
a particular area, it will defend it fiercely
against intruders. This area is the
gerbil's territory.

If you already have adult gerbils, you must
never try to put a new adult in their cage.
They might accept a new young gerbil, but
it must be introduced slowly and carefully.

Introducing a young gerbil

Thoroughly clean your gerbil's
cage and put in fresh
bedding. Place a
wire mesh panel
in the middle.

*The wire
mesh should
divide the
cage in two.*

Put the new gerbil on one side of the mesh
and the older gerbil on the other, so they
can see and smell each other.

These gerbils are meeting for the first time. They sniff to learn each other's scents.

Make sure the gerbils can't wriggle under the mesh, or through it.

Each day, switch the two gerbils around. After a few weeks, you should be able to remove the mesh completely.

47

Playtime

Gerbils love exploring and playing with a variety of toys. It's best to change the toys regularly, or the gerbils might become bored.

Cardboard tubes

Gerbils love tunnels. Give them the cardboard middle from the inside of a roll of toilet paper or of paper towels.

This boot-shaped toy has holes for the gerbil to poke its head through.

They will have hours of fun running through a cardboard tube and chewing it to bits.

Wheels

If you can't let your gerbils run around outside their cage, give them an exercise wheel. Avoid the kinds with gaps between the bars, as a gerbil's tail can easily get damaged in them.

A solid plastic wheel, like this one, is the safest kind for a gerbil.

You can adapt a wheel with gaps in to make it safe for your gerbils. Wind sticky tape all around the wheel, then spread bedding on the inside. Change the tape every few weeks.

Playing safe

You can let your gerbil out to run around, as long as you watch it closely. Keep it away from dangers such as hot radiators, electric cables, and liquids.

Gerbils are very inquisitive. They will investigate anything, even if it's not safe.

Warn people when your gerbil is out of its cage, so it doesn't get hurt accidentally. If you have lots of gerbils, it's safer to have only one out at once.

Exercise balls

You can let your gerbil run around outside its cage in a clear plastic exercise ball. Don't let it spend more than about 10 or 15 minutes in the ball, or it might become exhausted.

Exercise balls are useful if you don't have a room where your gerbils can safely run free.

Finding lost gerbils

If a gerbil escapes and you don't know which room it's in, put four sunflower seeds on the floor of each room. Close the doors, and see which seeds get eaten.

Sunflower seeds can usually lure lost gerbils out of hiding.

Baby gerbils

Baby gerbils are called pups. A male and female gerbil will have pups if they live together. It's best not to let this happen, as you'll need to find homes for all the pups.

The new mother

Female gerbils give birth to their pups after being pregnant for just 24 days. A mother gerbil can have up to seven pups at once.

This is what a nest of newborn pups looks like.

Newborn gerbils

Newborn gerbils are about the size of a grape.
They have no hair, and they can't see or hear.

For the first few
weeks, the pups stay
huddled in the nest
with their mother. She
licks them clean and
feeds them milk.

*A mother gerbil
cares for her pups.*

Separated parents

In the wild, gerbil parents stay together to
look after their pups. You should separate
pet gerbil parents before the birth,
though, or they will keep
having more pups.

*Just one pair
of gerbils could
produce around 50
pups in a year.*

Tiny explorers

Although they are blind, gerbil pups like to crawl around and explore. Their mother picks them up gently in her mouth and returns them to the nest if they stray too far.

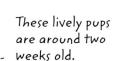

These lively pups are around two weeks old.

Growing up

The pups change quickly. Within two weeks, their fur has grown, their eyes are starting to open, and they can hear and run. At this age, they love to chase and wrestle with each other.

Pups like to play-fight, but they don't hurt each other.

Becoming parents

Most gerbils will start having pups when they are around four months old, but they can start earlier.

To avoid this, brothers and sisters must be separated from each other when they are around six weeks old.

This six-week-old gerbil already looks like a mini version of its mother.

If the pups stay with their parents, then they won't have pups of their own, but will help to care for any more babies their parents have.

Keeping healthy

Well-cared-for gerbils will rarely become sick. If you suspect something is wrong with your gerbil, you might be able to treat it at home, although some problems will need a vet.

Bald spots

Bald spots around a gerbil's nose are usually caused by it rubbing its face against the cage bars. If the skin looks red and runny, though, it might be allergic to its bedding, so try using a different kind.

If your gerbil rubs its nose a lot, like this, it might have an allergy.

Pests

Tiny mites can get in a gerbil's fur and make it itch. If you see movement in the fur, or sore skin, go to a pet store and buy a special lotion to kill the pests.

These mites are drawn close up, but are too small to see in real life. Check for sore patches of skin instead.

You must also wash the cage or tank with hot, soapy water, and replace the bedding.

A damaged tail

Gerbils' tails are fragile. Picking up a gerbil by its tail might break off the skin or the tuft on the end. A broken tail heals quickly, but never grows back to its full length.

A gerbil can survive losing part of its tail, but it will find it a little harder to balance.

Signs of sickness

Refusing food might mean that your gerbil is sick.

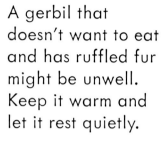

A gerbil that doesn't want to eat and has ruffled fur might be unwell. Keep it warm and let it rest quietly.

ACHOOO

If your gerbil's breathing makes a clicking sound, it probably has a cold. Take it to a vet right away.

A gerbil with a cold will sneeze and have trouble breathing.

Watery droppings are usually a sign of an upset tummy.

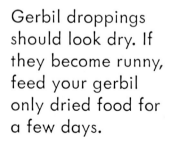

Gerbil droppings should look dry. If they become runny, feed your gerbil only dried food for a few days.

Weight problems

A gerbil that eats too much and exercises too little will get fat.

Give an overweight gerbil low-fat foods, such as dried peas.

If your gerbil is getting too thin, there might be a problem with its teeth. Overgrown teeth can be clipped. Broken teeth will grow back.

Older gerbils

As gerbils age, they sleep more and exercise less. When your gerbil is three years old, start adding a little vitamin powder to its food to help it stay healthy.

With a healthy diet and lots of exercise, your gerbil could live to be five years old, like this one.

Going to the vet

If your gerbil becomes sick and doesn't begin to recover by itself, it will need to see a vet.

On the move

Take your gerbil to the vet in a small, plastic carrying box. Avoid cardboard boxes, because your gerbil will be able to chew through them.

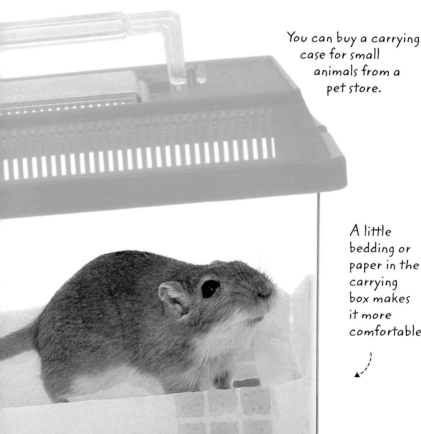

You can buy a carrying case for small animals from a pet store.

A little bedding or paper in the carrying box makes it more comfortable.

This gerbil is being sprayed with an anti-flea treatment.

The vet holds the gerbil by the base of its tail while she sprays its body.

What will the vet do?

Depending on what's wrong with your pet, the vet might give it an injection, or some medicine. Vets can also treat gerbils that have skin problems, or pests in their fur.

Teething troubles

If your gerbil's teeth have become overgrown, ask the vet to clip them. Overgrown teeth could harm your pet.

A gerbil's teeth grow too long if it doesn't have enough hard things to gnaw.

61

Going away

Gerbils can be left alone for a couple of nights, but if you're going away for longer, ask a friend to look after your pets.

A short break

If you're only away for a night or two, clean the gerbils' cage or tank and replace all the bedding. Fill the water bottle, and leave enough dry food to last until you return.

Don't leave fresh food, as it will spoil.

This jird is enjoying having a peanut as a treat while its owner is away.

Gerbilsitting

It's easier to ask someone you trust to visit your home, rather than trying to take a tank or large cage to them.

Leave your friend everything she will need to look after your pets. Tell her what sorts of food they can have.

Make sure your friend knows what to do if a gerbil escapes, and give her the phone number of a local vet.

Your friend can ask the vet for advice before taking the gerbil to see him. ╌╌▸

Index

Cover design by Kate Rimmer
Digital manipulation by Keith Furnival

Photo credits

(t-top, m-middle, b-bottom, l-left, r-right)
All photographs by Jane Burton, except
Front Cover bm © Jane Burton/Warren Photographic Ltd;
Front Cover br © Jane Burton/naturepl.com; 12b © SAVIC